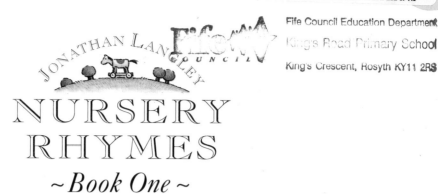

NURSERY RHYMES

~ Book One ~

JONATHAN LANGLEY

NURSERY RHYMES

~ *Book One* ~

Illustrated by Jonathan Langley

PictureLions
An Imprint of HarperCollins*Publishers*

Nursery Rhymes Book One is a selection
of rhymes and illustrations from
The Collins Book of Nursery Rhymes,
first published in hardback by
William Collins Sons & Co Ltd 1990
10 9 8 7 6 5 4 3 2
Copyright text and illustrations
© William Collins Sons and Co 1981, 1990

This selection published in Picture Lions 1992
Picture Lions is an imprint of
the Children's Division,part of
HarperCollins Publishers Ltd,
77–85 Fulham Palace Road,
Hammersmith, London, W6 8JB

Printed in Great Britain by
BPCC Hazell Books, Paulton and Aylesbury

CONTENTS

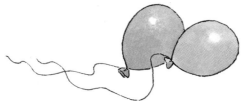

Nursery Days

Bye, baby bunting,
Daddy's gone a-hunting,
Gone to get a rabbit skin
To wrap the baby bunting in.

Pat-a-cake, pat-a-cake, baker's man,
Bake me a cake as fast as you can;
Pat it and prick it, and mark it with B,
Put it in the oven for Baby and me.

Dance to your daddy,
  My little babby,
Dance to your daddy,
  My little lamb.

You shall have a fishy
  In a little dishy,
You shall have a fishy
  When the boat comes in.

You shall have an apple,
  You shall have a plum,
You shall have a rattle-basket
  When your daddy comes home.

Hush-a-bye, baby, on the tree top,
When the wind blows, the cradle will rock;
When the bough breaks, the cradle will fall,
And down will come baby, cradle and all.

How many days has my baby to play?
Saturday, Sunday, Monday,
  Tuesday, Wednesday, Thursday, Friday,
Saturday, Sunday, Monday.
    Hop away, skip away,
    My baby wants to play;
My baby wants to play every day!

1 2 3 4 5

One to Ten, and Then Again

One, two, three,
I love coffee,
And Billy loves tea,
How good you be,
One, two, three,
I love coffee,
And Billy loves tea.

One, two, three, four, five,
Once I caught a fish alive,
Six, seven, eight, nine, ten,
Then I let it go again.
Why did you let it go?
Because it bit my finger so.
Which finger did it bite?
The little finger on the right.

11 12 13 14 15

6 7 8 9 10

One, two,
　　Buckle my shoe;
Three, four,
　　Knock at the door;
Five, six,
　　Pick up sticks;
Seven, eight,
　　Lay them straight;
Nine, ten,
　　A big fat hen;
Eleven, twelve,
　　Dig and delve;
Thirteen, fourteen,
　　Maids a-courting;
Fifteen, sixteen,
　　Maids in the kitchen;
Seventeen, eighteen,
　　Maids in waiting;
Nineteen, twenty,
　　My plate's empty.

16 17 18 19 20

I Saw a Ship a-Sailing

I saw a ship a-sailing,
A-sailing on the sea,
And oh, but it was laden
With pretty things for thee!

There were comfits in the cabin,
And apples in the hold;
The sails were made of silk,
And the masts were all of gold.

The four-and-twenty sailors,
That stood between the decks,
Were four-and-twenty white mice
With chains about their necks.

The captain was a duck
With a packet on his back,
And when the ship began to move
The captain said, Quack! Quack!

Down on the Farm

Come, butter, come,
Come, butter, come,
Peter stands at the gate
Waiting for a butter cake.
Come, butter, come.

Little Bo-peep has lost her sheep,
And doesn't know where to find them;
Leave them alone, and they'll come home,
Bringing their tails behind them.

If I had a donkey that wouldn't go,
Would I beat him? Oh no, no.
I'd put him in the barn and give him some corn,
The best little donkey that ever was born.

Baa, baa, black sheep,
　Have you any wool?
Yes, sir, yes, sir,
　Three bags full;
One for the master,
　And one for the dame,
And one for the little boy
　Who lives down the lane.

Cherry Stone Rhymes

Who shall I marry?

Tinker,
Tailor,
Soldier,
Sailor,
Rich man,
Poor man,
Beggar man,
Thief.

When will it be?

This year,
Next year,
Sometime,
Never.

Where shall I marry?

Church,
Chapel,
Cathedral,
Abbey.

And the ring?

Gold,
Silver,
Copper,
Brass.

How shall I get there?

Coach,
Carriage,
Wheelbarrow,
Dustcart.

What shall I wear?

Silk,
Satin,
Cotton,
Rags.

And where shall we live happily ever after?

Big house,
Little house,
Pig sty,
Barn.

What's for Dinner?

Polly put the kettle on,
Polly put the kettle on,
Polly put the kettle on,
  We'll all have tea.

Sukey take it off again,
Sukey take it off again,
Sukey take it off again,
  They've all gone away.

Davy Davy Dumpling,
  Boil him in the pot;
Sugar him and butter him,
  And eat him while he's hot.

Little Tommy Tucker
  Sings for his supper:
What shall we give him?
  White bread and butter.
How shall he cut it
  Without e'er a knife?
How will he be married
  Without e'er a wife?

Little Miss Muffet
Sat on a tuffet,
Eating her curds and whey;
There came a big spider,
Who sat down beside her
And frightened Miss Muffet away.

Pease porridge hot,
Pease porridge cold,
Pease porridge in the pot
Nine days old.
Some like it hot,
Some like it cold,
Some like it in the pot
Nine days old.

9 DAYS OLD

Jack Sprat could eat no fat,
  His wife could eat no lean,
And so between them both, you see,
  They licked the platter clean.

Rain, Rain, Go Away!

Blow, wind, blow!
And go, mill, go!
That the miller may grind his corn;
That the baker may take it,
And into bread make it,
And bring us a loaf in the morn.

March winds and April showers
Bring forth May flowers.

Rain, rain, go away,
Come again another day,
Little Johnny wants to play.

Ipsey Wipsey spider
    Climbing up the spout;
Down came the rain
    And washed the spider out:
Out came the sunshine
    And dried up all the rain;
Ipsey Wipsey spider
    Climbing up again.

A sunshiny shower
Won't last half an hour.

Rain on the green grass,
    And rain on the tree,
Rain on the house-top,
    But not on me.

I'm the king of the castle,
Get down you dirty rascal.

I'll sing you a song,
Nine verses long,
    For a pin;
Three and three are six,
And three are nine;
You are a fool,
    And the pin is mine.

Tell tale tit,
Your tongue shall be split
And all the little puppy dogs,
Shall have a little bit!

Finders keepers,
Losers weepers.

Here am I,
   Little Jumping Joan;
When nobody's with me
   I'm all alone.

Lucy Locket lost her pocket,
   Kitty Fisher found it;
Not a penny was there in it,
   Only ribbon round it.

The Toy Cupboard

Little John Jiggy Jag,
He rode a penny nag,
     And went to Wigan to woo:
When he came to a beck,
He fell and broke his neck,
     Johnny, how dost thou now?

I made him a hat
Of my coat lap,
     And stockings of pearly blue;
A hat and a feather,
To keep out cold weather,
     So, Johnny, how dost thou now?

Jerry Hall,
He is so small,
A rat could eat him,
Hat and all.

I had a little moppet,
I kept it in my pocket
And fed it on corn and hay;
There came a proud beggar
And said he would wed her,
And stole my little moppet away.

Hush baby, my doll, I pray you don't cry,
And I'll give you some bread and some milk by and
    by;
Or, perhaps you like custard, or may be a tart,
Then to either you're welcome, with all my whole
    heart.

All the Fun of the Fair

Smiling girls, rosy boys,
Come and buy my little toys;
Monkeys made of gingerbread,
And sugar horses painted red.

As I was going to Banbury,
  Upon a summer's day,
My dame had butter, eggs, and fruit,
  And I had corn and hay.
Joe drove the ox, and Tom the swine,
  Dick took the foal and mare;
I sold them all, then home to dine,
  From famous Banbury fair.

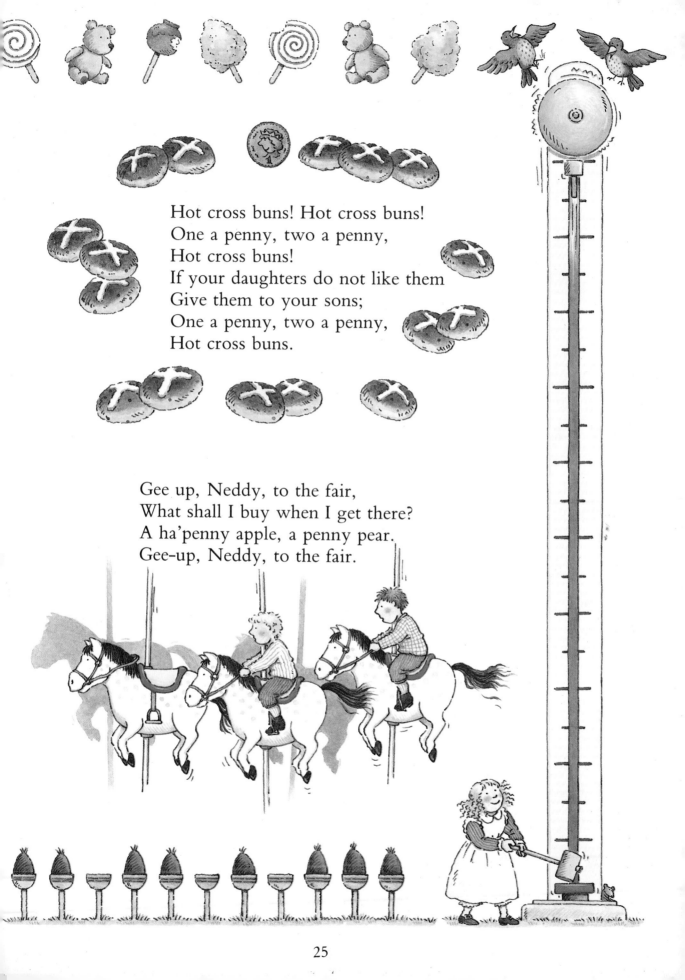

Hot cross buns! Hot cross buns!
One a penny, two a penny,
Hot cross buns!
If your daughters do not like them
Give them to your sons;
One a penny, two a penny,
Hot cross buns.

Gee up, Neddy, to the fair,
What shall I buy when I get there?
A ha'penny apple, a penny pear.
Gee-up, Neddy, to the fair.

Join Hands!

Poor Mary lies a-weeping, a-weeping, a-weeping,
Poor Mary lies a-weeping, on a bright summer's day!

Oh, why is she a-weeping, a-weeping, a-weeping?
Oh, why is she a-weeping, on a bright summer's day?

She's weeping for her true love, her true love, her true love,
She's weeping for her true love, on a bright summer's day.

On the carpet she must kneel,
Till the grass grows in the field,
Stand up now, upon your feet,
Choose the one you love so sweet!

Now you're married we wish you joy,
First the girl, and then the boy.
Kiss her once, kiss her twice,
Kiss her three times over!

Ring-a-ring o'roses,
A pocket full of posies,
    A-tishoo! A-tishoo!
We all fall down.

The cows are in the meadow
Lying fast asleep,
    A-tishoo! A-tishoo!
We all get up again.

Over Land and Sea

Over the water and over the lea,
  And over the water to Charlie.
I'll have none of your nasty beef,
  Nor I'll have none of your barley,
But I'll have some of your very best flour
  To make a white cake for my Charlie.

My mother sent me for some water,
For some water from the sea,
My foot slipped, and in I tumbled,
Three jolly sailors came to me:
One said he'd buy me silks and satins,
One said he'd buy me a guinea gold ring,
One said he'd buy me a silver cradle
For to rock my baby in.

If all the world was paper,
    And all the sea was ink,
If all the trees were bread and cheese,
    What should we have to drink?

Little Tee Wee,
He went to sea
In an open boat:
And while afloat
The little boat bended,
And my story's ended.

If all the seas were one sea,
    What a great sea that would be!
If all the trees were one tree,
    What a great tree that would be!
And if all the axes were one axe,
    What a great axe that would be!
And if all the men were one man,
    What a great man that would be!
And if the great man took the great axe,
    And cut down the great tree,
And let it fall into the great sea,
    What a splish-splash *that* would be!

Good Night

Down with the lambs,
Up with the lark,
Run to bed children
Before it gets dark.

Good night, God bless you,
Go to bed and undress you.

Good night, sweet repose,
Half the bed and all the clothes.

Come, let's to bed,
Says Sleepy-head;
Tarry a while, says Slow;
Put on the pot,
Says Greedy-gut,
We'll sup before we go.

Rock-a-bye, baby,
    Thy cradle is green,
Father's a nobleman,
    Mother's a queen;
And Betty's a lady,
    And wears a gold ring;
And Johnny's a drummer,
    And drums for the king.

Go to bed first,
A golden purse;
Go to bed second,
A golden pheasant;
Go to bed third,
A golden bird.

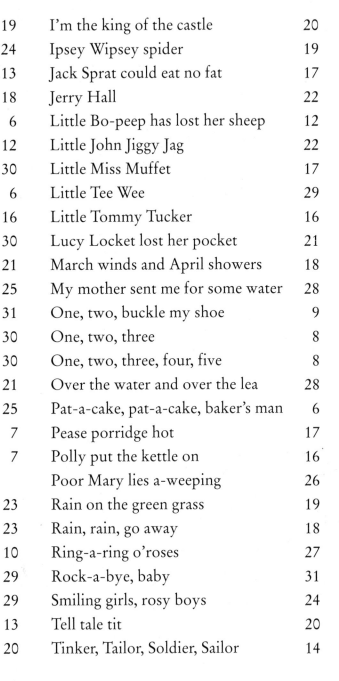

INDEX OF FIRST LINES